A New Dimension

How to be filled with the Holy Spirit

David Petts

© **Copyright: David Petts 2015**

All Rights Reserved. No part of this publication may be reproduced, stored in a retrieval system, or transmitted in any form or by any means – electronic, mechanical, photocopying, recording or otherwise – without prior permission from the author.

ISBN: 978-1-326-25308-0

This edition: 2015

Available from:

www.davidpetts.org

John baptised with water, but in a few days you will be baptised with the Holy Spirit (Acts 1:5)

You will receive power when the Holy Spirit comes on you; and you will be my witnesses in Jerusalem, and in all Judea and Samaria, and to the ends of the earth (Acts 1:8)

When the day of Pentecost came, they were all together in one place. Suddenly a sound like the blowing of a violent wind came from heaven and filled the whole house where they were sitting. They saw what seemed to be tongues of fire that separated and came to rest on each of them. All of them were filled with the Holy Spirit and began to speak in other tongues as the Spirit enabled them (Acts 2:1-4)

Repent and be baptised, every one of you, in the name of Jesus Christ for the forgiveness of your sins. And you will receive the gift of the Holy Spirit (Acts 2:38)

About this book

If you've just become a Christian, or even if you've been a Christian for some time, and you want to know more about the power of the Holy Spirit, then this book has been written for you. I've purposely written it in clear, almost chatty, English, so that it will be easy for even a young Christian to read and understand. It's meant to be a simple guide to what it means to be filled with the Holy Spirit.

We begin in the Book of Acts by looking at the last thing Jesus said to his disciples before he returned to Heaven. We look at what Acts teaches us about what it means to be filled with the Spirit and why it's important. We ask how we can know if we've been filled with the Spirit and talk about its relationship with speaking in tongues. Finally we look at what the Bible has to say about how we can, like those early disciples, be filled with the Holy Spirit and what to do once we have received.

Those who want a more detailed or academic discussion of the subject are invited to investigate some of the other books I've written on the subject. You will find a brief description of these at the end of this book or by visiting my website:

www.davidpetts.org

Jesus' last words

The wonderful story of the life of Jesus is recorded for us in the four Gospels. They tell us of his life, his teaching, and his miracles. They show us how he died on the cross to save us from our sins and how he rose again three days later. They record how, over a period of forty days, he showed himself to his disciples on many occasions so that there would be absolutely no doubt that he really was alive.

In the Book of Acts we read how finally, just before he left them and returned to heaven, he told them what he required them to do after he had gone. They were to go into all the world and tell everyone the good news about him. But before they did this they were to wait until they received the power of the Holy Spirit. This is what it tells us in Acts 1:

> *On one occasion, while Jesus was eating with them, he gave them this command: 'Do not leave Jerusalem, but wait for the gift my Father promised, which you have heard me speak about. For John baptised with water, but in a few days you will be baptised with the Holy Spirit'…*
>
> **…you will receive power when the Holy Spirit comes on you;** *and you will be my witnesses in*

Jerusalem, and in all Judea and Samaria, and to the ends of the earth'. After he said this, he was taken up before their very eyes, and a cloud hid him from their sight (Acts 1:4-5, 8-9).

So the disciples went back to Jerusalem as Jesus had commanded them and continued together in prayer until the Holy Spirit came. Then in Acts 2 we read:

When the day of Pentecost came, they were all together in one place. Suddenly a sound like the blowing of a violent wind came from heaven and filled the whole house where they were sitting. They saw what seemed to be tongues of fire that separated and came to rest on each of them. **All of them were filled with the Holy Spirit** *and began to speak in other tongues as the Spirit enabled them (Acts 2:1-4).*

So the promise that Jesus had made them was fulfilled. He had told them to wait for the gift that God had promised (Acts 1:4) and that they would be baptised in the Holy Spirit (Acts 1:5). This would be the power of the Holy Spirit coming on them empowering them to be witnesses to the ends of the earth (Acts 1:8). Luke tells us that this happened on the day of Pentecost when the disciples were filled with the Holy Spirit and began to speak languages they had never learned (Acts 2:4)[1].

As a result of this amazing miracle, a large crowd gathered and, after Peter had preached the gospel to them, over 3000 people were added to the church. (If you're not familiar with the details, you can read what happened in the rest of Acts 2). The Book of Acts goes on to tell us how, through the power of the Holy Spirit, thousands more people became Christians and churches were established throughout the then-known world. But let's look a bit more closely at what it meant for those early followers of Jesus to be filled with the Spirit.

---

[1] It's interesting to note that in the verses we've already looked at Luke uses four different expressions to refer to **the same thing**:

- o   Receiving the gift the Father had promised (1:4)
- o   Being baptised in the Holy Spirit (1:5)
- o   Receiving the power of the Spirit coming upon you (1:8)
- o   Being filled with the Spirit (2:4).

Later on he also uses

- o   Receiving (the gift of) the Holy Spirit

in the same way. See Acts 2:38, 8:15, 8:17, 8:19, 10:47, 19:2.

Filled with the Spirit – what does it mean?

It's not the same as becoming a Christian

The first thing to notice is that when the disciples were filled with the Spirit on the day of Pentecost they were already followers of Jesus. Their experience of the Spirit that day was not what made them Christians. They had already left all to follow Jesus (Matthew 19:27). They had confessed that he was the Christ, the son of the living God (Matthew 16:16). He had told them that they were already clean (John 15:3) and that their names were written in Heaven (Luke 10:20). But until Pentecost they were not yet filled with the Spirit.

We see something similar when we look at the Samaritans who were converted through Philip's preaching in Acts 8. They had believed Philip as he had preached the gospel to them and they had been baptised (v. 12), but the Holy Spirit had not yet 'come upon' any of them (v. 16)[2]. However, when Peter and John placed their hands on them (v.17), they received the Holy Spirit.

---

[2] It's important to remember here that in Acts expressions like 'the Spirit coming upon you' and 'being filled with the Spirit' are used interchangeably to mean the same thing. See footnote 1.

Other examples in Acts are the apostle Paul who was converted on the road to Damascus, but was not filled with the Spirit until Ananias had laid his hands on him (Acts 9:3-17) and the Ephesians in Acts 19:1-6. The Spirit came on them after Paul had baptised them in water after he had explained to them that it was Jesus who was the Christ about whom John the Baptist had told them.

All these examples show us that, when Luke uses expressions like 'being filled with the Spirit', 'receiving the Spirit', 'the Spirit coming upon a person', he is not talking about the work of the Holy Spirit in our lives which brings about our conversion. Being filled with the Spirit is different from being born again[3].

It's something that happens suddenly

The next thing to notice from the Book of Acts is that being filled with the Spirit is something that happens suddenly. Let's go back to the first few verses of Acts 2. For ten days the disciples had been waiting for the coming of the Holy Spirit. They were no more filled with the Spirit on the ninth day than they had been on the first day! But on the tenth day, the day of Pentecost, they

---

[3] I have written in more detail on this in *The Holy Spirit – an Introduction*. For more details, please see the books listed at the back of this book.

were suddenly (v. 2) filled with the Spirit (v. 4). This is clear from the use of the word 'suddenly' in verse 2 and from the tense of the Greek verb which Luke uses in verse 4, and the same is true of the verb used in Acts 4:31 when the disciples were filled again with the Holy Spirit[4].

Other examples in Acts include Acts 1:5 where Jesus promises his disciples that they will be 'baptised' in the Holy Spirit and Peter's statement in Acts 11:15 that the Holy Spirit 'fell on' Cornelius[5]. Falling seems to suggest something that happens suddenly and 'baptism' – always by immersion in the New Testament – can certainly not be administered gradually! This is important because some Christians have mistakenly confused being filled with the Spirit with the gradual process of sanctification that takes place in our lives day by day as we seek to become more like Jesus.

So being filled with the Spirit is a sudden experience that happens to us after we become Christians, but it's also important to understand that it's a supernatural experience.

---

[4] The verb 'filled' is in the Aorist Tense which is 'strictly the expression of a momentary or transient, single action' (Analytical Greek Lexicon, Bagster).

[5] The Greek verb means 'fell on' rather than 'came on' as in NIV.

It's a supernatural experience

We only need to read Acts 2:1-4 again to see that being filled with the Spirit is a supernatural experience. They saw supernatural tongues of fire, heard the supernatural wind of the Spirit, and spoke by supernatural power languages they had never learned. As we read on in Acts we see that by the same supernatural power of the Spirit they healed the sick (Acts 3, 5, 8, 9, 14, 19, 28), cast out demons (Acts 8, 16, 19) and even raised the dead (Acts 9, 20). The power of the Spirit they received at Pentecost, accompanied by speaking in tongues, was the gateway to other mighty gifts of the Spirit that resulted in thousands being won for Christ. And it's the same supernatural power of the Spirit that Christians need today if we are to win the world for Jesus!

But are these things for today or were they just for the early disciples as some Christians believe? The simple answer to this question is to be found in Acts 2:38-39 where Peter says to the crowd:

> *'Repent and be baptised, every one of you, in the name of Jesus Christ for the forgiveness of your sins. And you will receive the gift of the Holy Spirit.*
>
> *The promise is for you and your children and for all who are far off - for all whom the Lord our God will call'.*

This makes it clear that the gift of the Holy Spirit is available to all who will repent and be baptised. It was not just for those Peter was speaking to in Acts 2, but for their children and all those of future generations who would become Christians.

And as we read on in Acts we see this promise being fulfilled. The Spirit comes upon the Samaritans (Acts 8), on Paul (Acts 9), on the Roman centurion, Cornelius and his household (Acts 10), and on the Ephesians (Acts 19). These all had similar experiences to the disciples on the day of Pentecost and nowhere does the New Testament suggest that they are not for today. Indeed, the experience of millions of Christians alive today confirms that it is! What's more, the New Testament itself tells us to be filled with the Spirit (Ephesians 5:18). So, if Acts shows us what it's like to be filled with the Spirit, and if Ephesians tells us that we should be filled with the Spirit, doesn't that show that Christians today should expect a similar experience to what took place in the book of Acts? But that brings us to our next section. Why is it important to be filled with the Spirit?

The importance of being filled with the Spirit

Because JESUS believed it was important

Apart from the fact that God's word tells us to be filled with the Spirit (Ephesians 5:18), its importance is clear from what the Lord Jesus had to say about it. Let's look at Acts 1 again:

Acts 1:4

*On one occasion, while he was eating with them, he gave them this command: 'Do not leave Jerusalem, but **wait** for the gift my Father promised, which you have heard me speak about...'*

He says something similar in Luke 24:49

*'I am going to send you what my Father has promised; **but stay in the city** until you have been **clothed with power from on high'.*[6]

Of course we know that Jesus wanted his disciples to go and spread the good news about him all over the world. He, more than anyone else, cared about world evangelisation! He gave his life for it! He died to save us. So we might have expected him to tell his disciples start

---

[6] *Being clothed with power* is just another expression Luke uses to mean being baptised with or filled with the Holy Spirit.

preaching the good news straightaway. But he didn't. He told them to wait until they had received the power of God's Spirit.

But there's something else that shows us how important this was to Jesus. It was the last thing he said! It was the very last thing he talked about before he went back to Heaven. Let's look at Luke 24 again:

> 'I am going to send you what my Father has promised; but stay in the city until you have been clothed with power from on high'.
>
> When he had led them out to the vicinity of Bethany, he lifted up his hands and blessed them.
>
> While he was blessing them, he left them and was taken up into heaven (Luke 24:49-51).

Compare that with Acts 1:8-9:

> 'But you will receive power when the Holy Spirit comes on you; and you will be my witnesses in Jerusalem, and in all Judea and Samaria, and to the ends of the earth'.
>
> After he said this, he was taken up before their very eyes, and a cloud hid him from their sight.

In both these passages Jesus ascends into Heaven immediately after telling his disciples that they will need to receive the power of God's Spirit before they begin the task of world evangelisation.

Now we usually consider that a person's last words on earth are significant. How much more important, then, are the last words of our Lord Jesus Christ! And if Jesus' first disciples – who had spent three years with him, listening to his teaching, watching him work miracles, finally witnessing his death and resurrection – if they needed to be filled with the Spirit in order to spread the good news effectively, then how much more do we?

Because the apostles believed it was important

Certainly the early apostles had understood that what Jesus had said about this was important, because not only did they obey his instructions and wait until they had been filled with the Spirit before starting to preach the gospel, but they encouraged all new Christians to receive the same gift of the Holy Spirit. Notice what Peter says to the crowd on the day of Pentecost:

> *Peter replied, 'Repent and be baptised, every one of you, in the name of Jesus Christ for the forgiveness of your sins.* ***And you will receive the gift of the Holy Spirit.***

The promise is for you and your children and *for all who are far off –* ***for all whom the Lord our God will call'*** *(Acts 2:38-39).*

This shows us that all new Christians were expected to receive the power of God's Spirit enabling them to spread the good news to their own generation. This is also clear from a passage in Acts 8 which tells us what happened when the Samaritans became Christians:

When the apostles in Jerusalem heard that Samaria had accepted the word of God, they sent Peter and John to them.

When they arrived, they prayed for them that they might receive the Holy Spirit, because the Holy Spirit had not yet come upon any of them*; they had simply been baptised into the name of the Lord Jesus.*

Then Peter and John placed their hands on them, and ***they received the Holy Spirit*** *(Acts 8:14-17).*

These verses show us that although the Samaritans had become Christians, they had not yet received the Holy Spirit. What Luke means by this is clear from the expression he uses in verse 15 where he says that the Holy Spirit had not yet **come upon** any of them. In other words, they had not yet received the power that Jesus had promised in Acts 1:8 where he had said:

> *But you will receive power when the Holy Spirit **comes on** you; and you will be my witnesses in Jerusalem, and in all Judea and Samaria, and to the ends of the earth.*

The fact that the Samaritans had not yet received this power was so important to the apostles in Jerusalem that they sent Peter and John to them to lay hands on them and pray for them to receive it. And the apostle Paul was also aware of its great importance as is made clear in Acts 19:2 where the very first thing he says to the Ephesian disciples is:

> *'Did you receive the Holy Spirit when you believed?'*

So Jesus and the apostles believed that being filled with the Spirit was important. But why?

The answer is given in two of the passages that we have already looked at. The first is Acts 1:8 (which is already quoted at the top of this page). The second is Acts 2:4 where we read:

> *All of them were filled with the Holy Spirit and began to speak in other tongues as the Spirit enabled them.*

Acts 1:8 shows us that it's important because it gives us power to be witnesses. Acts 2:4 shows us that that power is manifested in supernatural gifts like speaking in tongues. Being filled with the Spirit is important because it's the gateway to spiritual gifts. And in Acts it was spiritual gifts like tongues and healings and miracles that made evangelism powerfully effective!

But that leads us to another question:

How do we know if we've received this power of the Holy Spirit?

How do I know I've received?

Since Ephesians 5:18 tells us to be filled with the Spirit, it is clearly very important to know whether we have been filled with the Spirit or not. In this connection it is particularly important that we should hear what the Bible has to say rather than just listening to the testimony of others or relying on our own opinions or feelings. As we shall see, the Bible is extremely clear on the matter. The first thing to notice is that we are definitely right to expect some form of evidence.

Evidence is to be expected

Some people have the idea that we know that we have received the Spirit by some kind of 'inner witness' or feeling, but this certainly has no basis in the New Testament. Acts makes it quite plain that New Testament Christians were expected to know whether they had 'received the Spirit' or not.

In Acts 2 it is very clear from Luke's description of the events which took place at Pentecost that those first disciples knew that they had been filled with the Spirit. Indeed the evidence that a person had been filled with the Spirit[7] was so clear that the apostles could tell the church in Acts 6:3 to choose seven men known to be full of the Spirit when they needed to give them the responsibility for the daily distribution of food.

The fact that in Acts 8:18 Simon saw that through the laying on of the apostles' hands the Holy Spirit was given is further proof that there was visible evidence of the Spirit's coming.

In Acts 10:44-46 we are told that Peter and his companions knew that the Gentiles had received the Spirit because they heard them speaking in tongues, and in Acts 19:1-7, Paul's very question, Did you receive the Holy Spirit when you believed? clearly implies that the Ephesians would have known whether they had received the Spirit or not.

In short, Acts makes it very clear that some form of evidence is to be expected when a person receives the Spirit. But what evidence exactly?

---

[7]Please remember that *being filled with the Spirit, being baptised with the Spirit, receiving the Spirit, etc.,* are interchangeable expressions - see footnote 1.

What evidence is to be expected?

To answer this question we must turn to the passages in Acts where Luke describes what happens when people receive the Holy Spirit. These are:

- o The day of Pentecost (Acts 2:1-4)
- o The Samaritans (8:14-24)
- o Cornelius and his household (10:44-48)
- o The Ephesians (19:1-7).

In his description of the Day of Pentecost Luke records three distinct supernatural phenomena:

*When the day of Pentecost came they were all together in one place. Suddenly **a sound like the blowing of a violent wind** came from heaven and filled the whole house where they were sitting. They saw what seemed to be **tongues of fire** that separated and came to rest on each of them. All of them were filled with the Holy Spirit and began to **speak in other tongues** as the Spirit enabled them (Acts 2:1-4).*

Of these three supernatural phenomena two took place before the disciples were filled with the Spirit. Only one, speaking in tongues, is recorded as a direct result of their having been filled. Further, it is noteworthy that this was the experience of them all. If there were some 120 people present (see Acts 1:15), then this passage records not one, but 120 cases of people being filled with the Spirit! And the direct and immediate result was that each person filled was enabled to speak in tongues.

This strongly suggests that speaking in tongues is the evidence that we should expect to indicate that a person has been filled with the Spirit. This is further confirmed a few verses later. Amazed by the disciples' ability to speak languages they have not learned, the crowd ask:

> *Are not all these men who are speaking Galileans? Then how is it that each of us hears them in his own native language? ... What does **this** mean? (Acts 2:7 and 12)*

to which Peter replies:

> ***This** is what was spoken by the prophet Joel, 'In the last days, says God, I will pour out my Spirit on all people....'*   *(Acts 2:16-17).*

Here it is important to realise that Peter's answer must be understood in the light of the crowd's question. The question was about tongues. It was therefore about tongues that Peter was speaking when he replied and quoted the prophecy from Joel. The speaking in tongues about which the crowd was asking was the sign that

God's promise had been fulfilled. The Spirit was now poured out upon all people.

Now with regard to the case of the Samaritans recorded in Acts 8, verse 18 tells us that Simon saw that the Holy Spirit was given to the Samaritans (v. 18) but we are not told what he saw. However, although there is no explicit mention of speaking in tongues in this passage, the IVF New Bible Dictionary confirms that tongues 'was doubtless one of the visible manifestations among the earliest Samaritan believers'[8].

However, it is worth noting that by not telling us precisely what Simon saw, Luke is clearly indicating that this passage is not intended to be a full description of what happened. The most we can learn from it is that we should expect visible evidence when people receive the Spirit. It offers no clear indication as to what that evidence might be and so our conclusion must be drawn from the other three passages, all of which do offer a very full description of events.

This brings us to the case of Cornelius in Acts 10 where we read:

> *While Peter was still speaking these words, the Holy Spirit came on all who heard the message.*

---

[8] New Bible Dictionary, London, IVF, 1962, p. 1286

> *The circumcised believers who had come with Peter were astonished that the gift of the Holy Spirit had been poured out even on the Gentiles.*
>
> *For they heard them speaking in tongues and praising God* (Acts 10:44-46).

Here there are no manifestations of the wind and fire that happened at Pentecost. Yet Peter and his companions knew that Cornelius and his household had received the Spirit simply because they heard them speak in tongues (v. 46). Peter refers to this again in the next chapter when he says:

> *As I began to speak, the Holy Spirit came on them as he had come on us at the beginning. Then I remembered what the Lord had said, 'John baptised with water, but you will be baptised with the Holy Spirit'. So if God gave them the same gift as he gave us ... who was I to think that I could oppose God?' (Acts 11:15-17).*

Putting these two passages together, we see that Peter knew that Cornelius and his household had been baptised in the Spirit[9] because he heard them speak in tongues, just as he and the other disciples had done at Pentecost.

---

[9] Please remember that 'baptised with the Spirit' and 'filled with the Spirit' refer to the same experience. See footnote 1.

Finally, in Acts 19:1-7, we read how twelve Ephesians received the Spirit. Once Paul had baptised them into the name of the Lord Jesus, he laid his hands on them and the Holy Spirit came on them and they spoke in tongues and prophesied.

It is significant that speaking in tongues is mentioned first here. The natural way to understand this is simply that it happened first. They spoke in tongues and then they prophesied. Understood this way the passage conforms to the other examples Luke has given us of disciples receiving the Spirit. **Wherever he gives us a full description, speaking in tongues is the first recorded event after people are filled with the Spirit.**

So the passages where Luke gives us a full description of people being baptised in the Spirit record some 150 baptisms in the Spirit (120 at Pentecost, a centurion's household in Caesarea, and about 12 in Ephesus). In each case the first recorded event is speaking in tongues. In the light of all this it is clear that Luke intends us to understand that when we are filled the Spirit for the first time we should expect to speak in tongues.

But what is the value of speaking in tongues?

The value of speaking in tongues

As we have already seen, when the disciples were filled with the Spirit on the day of Pentecost, they were able to speak languages[10] they had never learned. There were thousands of people from many different nations who had come to Jerusalem for the feast of Pentecost, and when they heard the disciples speaking in the different languages of the countries from which they had come, they were amazed and asked:

> *'Are not all these men who are speaking Galileans? Then how is it that each of us hears them in his own native language?*
>
> *...What does this mean?' (Acts 2:7, 8, 12).*

As a result of this miracle, and Peter's Spirit-empowered preaching that followed, some 3000 people were converted (Acts 2:41). In this case, speaking in tongues acted as a powerful sign to people who were not yet Christians and led to their giving their lives to Christ. This was something Jesus had promised would happen (Mark 16:17) and there are many examples of speaking in tongues being used in this way today. I personally had the experience of speaking in tongues in a meeting and

---

[10] 'Tongues' simply means 'languages'.

being told afterwards by a Gypsy woman that she had understood every word I had said and that I had been speaking Romany, a language used by the Gypsies when speaking among themselves. God had powerfully spoken to her through what I had said even though I had not understood a word I was saying!

So one great purpose of speaking in tongues is as a miraculous sign. But this is by no means the only way in which it is used, and in 1 Corinthians 14 Paul makes it clear that there is a value in speaking in tongues even when there is no-one present who can understand the language that's being spoken.

The first thing he tells us is that when we speak in tongues, we edify ourselves (v. 4). This means that we build ourselves up spiritually. Of course there are other ways we can be built up spiritually – by prayer, Bible reading, going to church, for example. So some Christians ask, 'Do I really need to speak in tongues?' But I have never really understood this question! If God has provided another way for us to grow spiritually, he must have a reason for it. And we don't say (I hope), 'I read my Bible, so I don't need to pray' or 'I pray, so I don't need to go to church'. No, we need all these things to help us grow in our Christian lives, and if God says that by speaking in tongues we build ourselves up, then why would we not want to speak in tongues?

Later in the same chapter Paul tells us that when we speak in tongues we are praying with our spirit. He says this:

'If I pray in a tongue, my spirit prays, but my mind is unfruitful.

So what shall I do? I will pray with my spirit, but I will also pray with my mind; I will sing with my spirit, but I will also sing with my mind' (1 Corinthians 14:14-15).

So, if I pray in tongues, I am praying with my spirit. But Paul also says that I should also pray with my mind. This means that if I pray in a language which I understand – for example, English – I am praying with my mind. But if I pray in a language which I do not understand – i.e. tongues – it is not my mind that is praying but my spirit. It was clearly very important to Paul that he should do both. We know that he valued very highly his ability to pray with his spirit by speaking in tongues, because in verse 18 he says:

I thank God that I speak in tongues more than all of you.

But he also realised the importance of praying with his mind, in a language he could understand (which in his case would have included Aramaic or Hebrew or Greek). So he makes clear to the Corinthians that he does both and in doing so is recommending that they should do the same. For English speaking people today this means that we should pray not only with our mind in English, but also with our spirit, in tongues. I find it interesting that the Bible tells us of no other way of praying with our spirit than by praying in tongues. That means then that the only way we can pray with our spirit is to pray in tongues, and since our spirit is such an important part of us – it is our spirit that lives on when we die – I cannot imagine why God should want some Christians to be able to pray with their spirit and others not to be able to! In other words, God wants all Christians to pray in tongues!

But, at first sight anyway, that seems to contradict something Paul says in 1 Corinthians 12:30 where he says:

Do all speak in tongues?

I have given a detailed answer to this in my book *The Holy Spirit – an Introduction*, but here it's enough to say that in 1 Corinthians 14 Paul makes it clear that there are two distinct uses of speaking in tongues. It can be used in our private devotions and it can be used in church. When it's used in church it requires interpretation so that other people can understand and be edified. When it's used in private, interpretation isn't necessary. Now it's clear from the context of Paul's question in 1 Corinthians

12:30 that it's the use of tongues in church that he's referring to, because his next question is, *Do all interpret?* So although not all Christians will speak in tongues in church, that does not mean that all should not do so privately.

But now let's look at one last benefit of speaking in tongues. It's clear from 1 Corinthians 14:14 where Paul says:

> *...if I pray in a tongue, my spirit prays, but my mind is unfruitful.*

In other words, when I pray in tongues I don't understand what I'm saying! Now it's quite likely that you're thinking, 'Well, what's the point of that?!' And that's a very reasonable question. But the answer is this: When I pray or praise God in a language I can't understand, I'm set free from the limitations of my English vocabulary!

It works like this. I can be at the top of a mountain looking around me at the majesty of God's creation and I really feel like praising the Lord! Now I can do that in English, but somehow I can't find the right words to express how wonderful God is. That's where speaking in tongues comes in. Immediately I'm set free from the limits of my mind and my spirit is free to praise God in words I don't understand, words inspired by the Holy Spirit.

On another occasion I might be asked to pray for someone who is terminally ill. Maybe they've been prayed for many times and yet there is no apparent answer. How am I to pray? I know that God is a healing God – I've seen him do it many times – but what I don't know is how and when he's going to heal[11]. Once again, this is where speaking in tongues can be very helpful. When I just don't know what to pray in English I'm glad I can trust the Holy Spirit to assist my prayers as I pray with my spirit by speaking in tongues. Maybe that's what Paul meant when he said:

We do not know what we ought to pray for, but the Spirit himself intercedes for us with groans that words cannot express (Romans 8:26).

So speaking in tongues is very valuable because:

- o It can be a powerful sign to those who are not yet Christians
- o When we speak in tongues we build ourselves up
- o When we speak in tongues we are praying with our spirit

---

[11] Healing is a big subject and we can't discuss it in detail here. If you want to know more, consider reading my book, *Just a Taste of Heaven – a biblical and balanced approach to God's healing power.*

- *When we speak in tongues we're set free from the limits of our English vocabulary.*

But now it's time to tell you how to get started!

How to get started

The Holy Spirit is a Gift

The first thing we need to understand is that the Holy Spirit is a gift. Jesus promised that our heavenly Father would **give** the Spirit to those who ask him (Luke 11:13) and Acts too frequently refers to the Spirit as a gift[12]. In this connection, it is important that we understand two things:

The gift cannot be earned

If the Holy Spirit is a gift then there is no way we can earn the right to receive him. Many Christians are held back from receiving the Spirit because of a sense of their own unworthiness. They feel the need to achieve a certain level of holiness before they will ask God for the gift of his Spirit. But Acts makes it clear that the Spirit was given to young converts. Their only holiness came from their repentance and faith in Christ.

It is of course true that we are not worthy to receive the Spirit. We never will be! But neither are we worthy to enter heaven. Our certainty of eternal life depends not on our own righteousness but on the fact that Jesus died for us. In response to our repentance and faith in what

---

[12]Acts 2:38, 5:32, 8:20, 10:45, 11:17

Christ did for us at Calvary, God has declared us righteous. He looks on us as though we had never sinned at all. That is what justification means. It is God who, by his grace, has made us fit for heaven, and because of his grace and forgiveness we may receive (not earn or merit) the gift of the Spirit[13].

The gift has already been given

And there is no longer any need for us to wait for the gift. It is true that before Pentecost the disciples were told to wait (Acts 1:4), but that was because the Spirit was not yet given (John 7:39). But at Pentecost the waiting period was over. The gift was given.

The child who has been promised a present for its birthday must wait to receive it. But when its birthday has come, there is no more waiting. The gift is there to be taken! In some ways Pentecost was the birthday of the Church and ever since, thank God, the gift has been there to be taken. After Pentecost we never find a single occasion when Christians waited for the gift of the Spirit.

---

[13]In Paul's writings the Spirit is seen as a foretaste of heaven. See for example Ephesians 1:13. For more about this, see *The Holy Spirit – an Introduction.*

The gift was, and is, available to all for at Pentecost the Spirit was poured out on all people (Acts 2:17)[14].

How to Receive the Gift

So how may we receive the gift? Acts 2:38 makes it clear that the promise is for all who will Repent and be baptised[15]. So what more must we do to receive the Spirit?

The answer to this question is found in John 7:37-38 where Jesus says:

> ... *'If anyone is thirsty, let him come to me and drink.*
>
> *Whoever believes in me, as the Scripture has said, streams of living water will flow from within him'.*

John then adds:

> *By this he meant the Spirit, whom those who believed in him were later to receive. Up to that time the Spirit*

---

[14] This does not mean, of course, that all people have received the Spirit. It signifies that as from Pentecost the Spirit, who previously had been given to relatively few chosen individuals for a specific purpose, was now available to all.

[15] People usually received the gift of the Spirit after being baptised in water. However, baptism must not be seen as an absolute condition for receiving the Spirit, as the case of Cornelius (Acts 10:44-48) makes clear. It is noteworthy, however, that he *was* baptised immediately after receiving the Spirit.

had not been given, since Jesus had not yet been glorified (v. 39).

This meant that once the Spirit had been given (at Pentecost) anyone who was thirsty might come to him and drink. The key here is coming to Jesus. He is the one who baptises with the Holy Spirit[16]. As we come to him, thirsty for the Spirit, we should come for cleansing if we need it, we should come expecting, and we should come in worship.

But before we look at each of these aspects a little more closely it is important to note that in the Book of Acts the Spirit was sometimes received through the laying on of hands.

The Laying on of Hands

As we look at the four incidents in Acts where we are told about groups of people receiving the Spirit[17], it is interesting to note that on two of these occasions the Spirit was received through the laying on of hands. It was through the laying on of the apostles' hands that the Samaritans received the Spirit (Acts 8:17-18), and the Spirit came on the Ephesians when Paul placed his hands on them (Acts 19:6). Indeed Paul himself was

---

[16]Matthew 3:11, Mark 1:8, Luke 3:16, John 1:33.

[17]Acts 2:4, 8:14ff, 10:44ff, 19:1-7.

filled with the Spirit when Ananias laid his hands on him (Acts 9:17) although Luke's account here is less detailed than in the other passages.

In fact it was only at Pentecost and at Caesarea that the Spirit was received without the laying on of hands and there were possibly special reasons for this on both occasions. Pentecost was the first occasion for Jesus' disciples to receive the Spirit and so there was no-one to lay hands on them. In the case of Cornelius those receiving the Spirit were Gentiles and the fact that the Spirit was given without the laying on of hands could well be understood as a further token that God had accepted them (Acts 10:47, 11:15-18).

So perhaps the usual means of receiving the Spirit is through the laying on of hands. However, people are sometimes filled with the Spirit without it if the Lord has some special purpose in their situation. Generally speaking, then, if you're seeking to be filled with the Spirit, I would encourage you to ask for the laying on of hands. As you do so, it will help if you come in the following way.

Come for cleansing

As we have already seen, we're not good enough in our own righteousness to receive God's Holy Spirit. But because of our faith in Christ we have been justified

(Romans 5:1). God has declared us righteous despite our unworthiness and it is only in that righteousness that we are fit to receive the Spirit.

Yet despite this we may well still feel the need for forgiveness as we come to Jesus asking him for the gift of the Spirit. In this connection it is always helpful to remember 1 John 1:9 which says:

> *If we confess our sin to him he will forgive us and cleanse us from all unrighteousness.*

If you're conscious of your need of forgiveness, claim that promise right now. Jesus really will cleanse you from all unrighteousness.

Come expecting

Now that you're freshly cleansed from your sin you may expect God to fill you with his Spirit. Jesus' promise in Luke 11 is a source of great encouragement here. The passage teaches us two main truths:

1) if we ask for the Holy Spirit God will give us the Holy Spirit

2) when as children of God we ask for the Spirit God will not let us receive 'stones' or 'scorpions' or 'snakes'.

So when we ask for the Spirit we must expect to receive the Spirit. Our heavenly Father won't let us get the wrong thing! He does not allow his children to receive harmful, counterfeit, or satanic gifts. He does not deal in demons! When his children ask for the Spirit, it is the Spirit he gives.

So ask for the Spirit and expect to receive and expect to speak in tongues. In this connection it may help you to consider the following verses:

> ...***they***...*began to speak in tongues (Acts 2:4).*
>
> *...they heard **them** speaking in tongues (Acts 10:46)*
>
> *... **they** spoke in tongues (Acts 19:6)*
>
> *If I pray in an unknown tongue, **my** spirit prays.. (1 Cor. 14:14)*

These verses show us that speaking in tongues is something you **do**, not something that happens to you! And it's not the Holy Spirit who speaks in tongues – **you** do. Nowhere does the Bible refer to the Holy Spirit speaking in tongues. He enables **us** to do so (Acts 2:4). He makes sure that the right sounds come out of our mouths. But it is **we** who speak in tongues, and it is when in faith we begin to praise God in this way that we begin to pray with the spirit as distinct from praying *with the mind*[18].

---

[18] 1 Corinthians 14:14ff

Come to Jesus in worship

The disciples who were filled with the Spirit on the day of Pentecost had spent time in prayer (Acts 1:14), but they had also spent time in worship (Luke 24:49-53). Jesus had told them that the Holy Spirit would come, and it seems that the disciples not only prayed for his coming but praised God that he would come. Jesus had said:

If I go, I will send him to you (John 16:7).

The source of the disciples' joy as they waited for the coming of the Holy Spirit was that Jesus had gone! They had seen him go. He had told them that they would be baptised in the Holy Spirit in a few days (Acts 1:5). They would receive power for witnessing when the Spirit came (v. 8). And then, he was taken up before their very eyes (v. 9). They saw him go into heaven (v. 11).

They had never seen him like this before! They had seen him as a carpenter, a teacher, a miracle-worker, even as the Messiah. They had come to see him as the Christ, the Son of the living God, and eventually, after his resurrection, as Lord and God. But always God upon earth. Now their gaze was lifted heavenward, far above all rule and authority, power and dominion, and every title that can be given, not only in the present age but also in the age to come!

Christ is ascended. He is King. He is Lord. He is God. He reigns in heaven, he reigns over the earth. All things are by him and through him and for him and to him. He is before all things and by him all things exist. Jesus of Nazareth is Lord of the universe! No wonder they worshipped!

Will you worship him? Worship him with your mind, but worship with your spirit too. Begin by faith to utter those new-found words of praise upon your lips. As you begin to speak, the Spirit will enable you. Yes, come to Jesus. Come for cleansing. Come expecting. Come in worship and adoration. Jesus is glorified. The Spirit has been given. If you are thirsty, come and drink!

Once you've received

Speak in tongues every day

Once you have been filled with the Spirit and started to speak in tongues, remember to do so every day. When you speak in tongues you are praying or praising God with your spirit and in doing so you are building yourself up spiritually. Notice Paul's determination when he says:

> *I **will** pray with my spirit, but I **will** also pray with my mind (1 Corinthians 14:14).*

In Ephesians 5:18 the command to be filled with the Spirit really means **Keep on** being filled with the Spirit. The fact that it's a command shows us that it's our responsibility. That's why Paul reminded Timothy to:

> ***fan into flame** the gift of God, which is in you through the laying on of my hands. For God did not give us a spirit of timidity, but a spirit of power, of love and of self-discipline (2 Timothy 1:6-7).*

It was up to Timothy to do this and it's our responsibility too. We can fan into flame the gift of God's Spirit within us by speaking in tongues every day.

Trust what Jesus said in Luke 11

As we've already seen, in Luke 11 Jesus promises that when God's children ask for the Holy Spirit, God won't give them 'stones' or 'snakes'. Sometimes, particularly with regard to speaking in tongues, we're tempted to doubt whether we've got 'the real thing'. Can those strange sounds I make when I speak in tongues really be another language? It's when we have doubts like this that we need to remember Jesus' promise – no stones or snakes! When God has given us a gift, Satan cannot take it away. But if he can convince us that the gift isn't real, he knows we'll stop using it! So trust what Jesus said in Luke 11.

Start to ask God for other spiritual gifts

Speaking in tongues is just the beginning. There are other supernatural gifts that the Holy Spirit can give us[19]. For example, the Ephesians in Acts 19 not only spoke in tongues when they were filled with the Spirit. They prophesied too. Peter and John were filled with the Spirit and spoke in tongues in Acts 2, but in Acts 3 they were used in the miraculous healing of a man who had never been able to walk. How wonderful it would be if God started to use you in this way!

---

[19] You'll find a list in 1 Corinthians 12:8-10. See my book *Body Builders* for more details.

As you ask for other gifts, remember that you can't tell the Holy Spirit what gifts to give you. Spiritual gifts are given as the Holy Spirit determines (1 Corinthians 12:11). He knows what's best. But keep filled with the Spirit day by day and he will lead you into the gifts that are right for you.

Tell others about Jesus

Finally, always remember that when Jesus promised his disciples that they would receive the Spirit's power, it was with a distinct purpose:

> *But you will receive power when the Holy Spirit comes on you; and you will be my witnesses in Jerusalem, and in all Judea and Samaria, and to the ends of the earth.*

As we read on in Acts we see how that power was demonstrated in amazing miracles which led to the conversion of many people. The same is true today. As you tell people about Jesus, ask the Holy Spirit to back up your testimony in some remarkable way. If they are obviously in some need, offer to pray for them. Even if you feel nervous, the Holy Spirit will strengthen you and lead you as you step out in faith. I can't tell you how he will use you, or what gifts he will give you. But I can tell you that God has a purpose in filling you with his Spirit and that he will use you and bless you as you witness for him.

Other helpful books by David Petts

If you'd like to explore this subject more, the following books are available from my website where a more detailed description of each book may be found.

The Holy Spirit – an Introduction

For a more detailed look at the person and work of the Holy Spirit this book is a must. It deals with the Spirit in the Old and New Testaments, the Spirit in the teaching of Jesus, the Spirit in the believer, the fruit and gifts of the Spirit, the Spirit in the church, and the Holy Spirit in the future.

Body Builders – gifts to make God's people grow

A detailed look at spiritual gifts in the New Testament, examining particularly the gifts listed in Ephesians 4:11 and those in 1 Corinthians 12:8-10. This book will help you understand what these gifts are and how to receive them.

Signs from Heaven – why I believe

A short book intended as an evangelistic tool containing testimonies of miracles from my own experience.

Just a Taste of Heaven – a biblical and balanced approach to God's healing power

As the title suggests, this book is about healing. Part One deals with biblical passages on healing. Part Two presents a positive but balanced theology of healing and Part Three offers practical guidelines for ministering to sick people with examples of miracles of healing from my own experience. If you want to be used in healing, I encourage you to read this book.

You'd Better Believe It!

20 chapters on basic Christian doctrine with study questions at the end of each chapter. Suitable for personal study or for use in home-groups.

How to Live for Jesus

Intended for new Christians, this book contains 10 short chapters on living the Christian life.

For more details on any of these books, visit:

www.davidpetts.org